# Chicano and Mexica

## Icons, Myths and Legends

### A Coloring Book for Adults

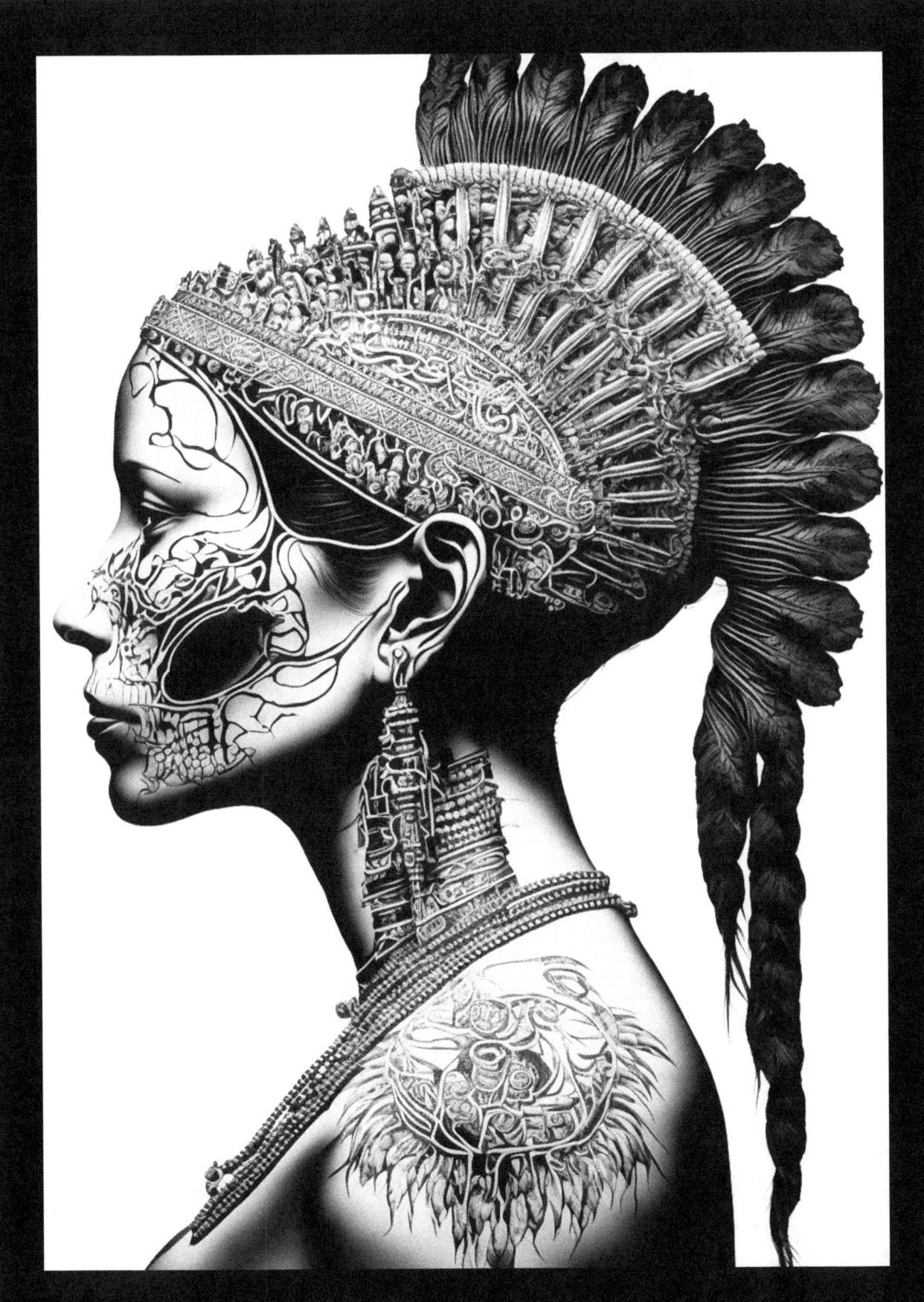

www.ingramcontent.com/pod-product-compliance
Lightning Source LLC
Chambersburg PA
CBHW080502220526
45465CB00006B/2355